D1405933

LET'S TALK ABOUT
BEING A
BAD SPORT

By Joy Berry

Illustrated by John Costanza

CHILDRENS PRESS ®

CHICAGO

13172N

Let's talk about BEING A BAD SPORT.

3

Bad sports
    are happy only
    when they win.

When bad sports lose they often
  pout,
  cry, or
  throw a tantrum.

7

Bad sports
tell lies to win.

Bad sports
cheat to win.

11

Bad sports
criticize others
to win.

13

Bad sports are not good winners.

They act as though they are
better than people who
have lost.

Bad sports say and do things to make the people who have lost feel bad.

17

No one likes to be with a bad sport.
Do not be one.
Try to be a good sport.

Good sports realize
no one wins all the time.

Sometimes you win.
Sometimes you lose.
Losing does not make you bad.
Winning does not make you good.

When good sports lose,
they congratulate the winner.

When good sports lose, they allow
the winner to enjoy winning.

Good sports try to make the winners feel
    they did well, and
    they deserved to win.

13172 N

North Street School

When good sports win,
   they try to make the people who have
   lost feel good.

When good sports win,
they are nice to the people who have lost.

Good sports encourage the people who have lost
to try again.

To be happy, treat others
the way you want to be treated.

Everyone is happier
when no one is a bad sport.

About the Author
Joy Berry is the author of more than 150 self-help books for children. She has advanced degrees and credentials in both education and human development and specializes in working with children from birth to twelve years of age. Joy is the founder of the Institute of Living Skills. She is the mother of a son, Christopher, and a daughter, Lisa.